DAD JOKES

awfully good dad jokes

A MESSAGE to DAD

_____

_____

_____

_____

 @DADJOKES1    @DADJOKES01

Copyright ©Dad Jokes: Awfully Good Dad Jokes
All rights reserved. This book or any portion
thereof may not be reproduced or used in any manner whatsoever
without the express written permission of the publisher except for the use of brief quotations in a book review.
Printed worldwide
First Printing, 2020

WWW.DADJOKESGIFT.COM

I FARTED IN AN ELEVATOR.

PEOPLE SAID IT WAS WRONG ON SO MANY LEVELS.

A POLICEMAN JUST TOLD ME MY DOGS ARE CHASING PEOPLE ON BIKES.

I'M JUST IMPRESSED THEY CAN REACH THE PEDALS.

WHY ARE CEMETERIES SO POPULAR?

PEOPLE ARE DYING to GET IN.

WHAT DID THE BUFFALO SAY WHEN it WAVED to its CHILD?

BISON!

WHAT IS THE LOUDEST PET IN THE WORLD?

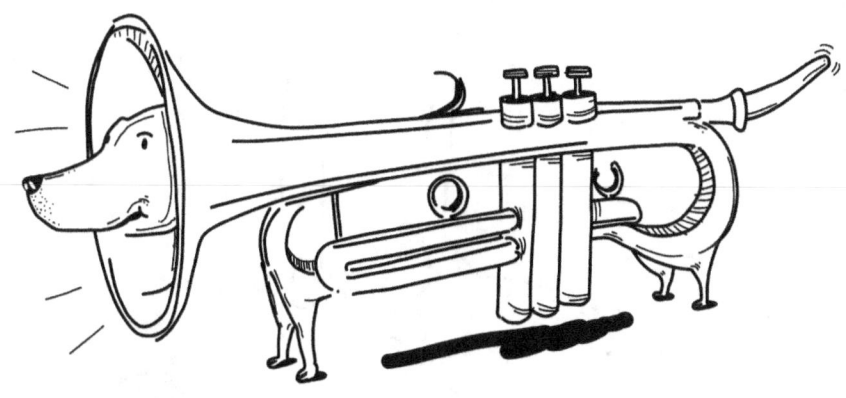

A TRUMPET.

I USED TO HATE FACIAL HAIR

BUT AFTER A WHILE IT GREW ON ME.

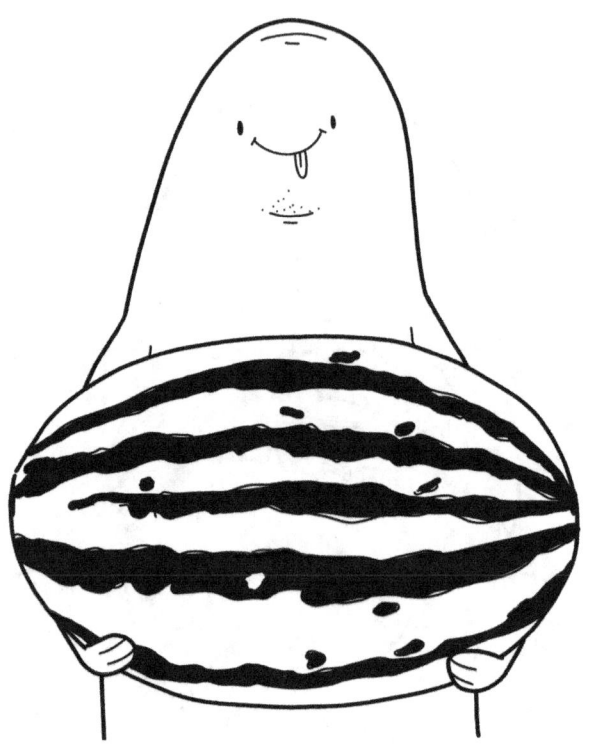

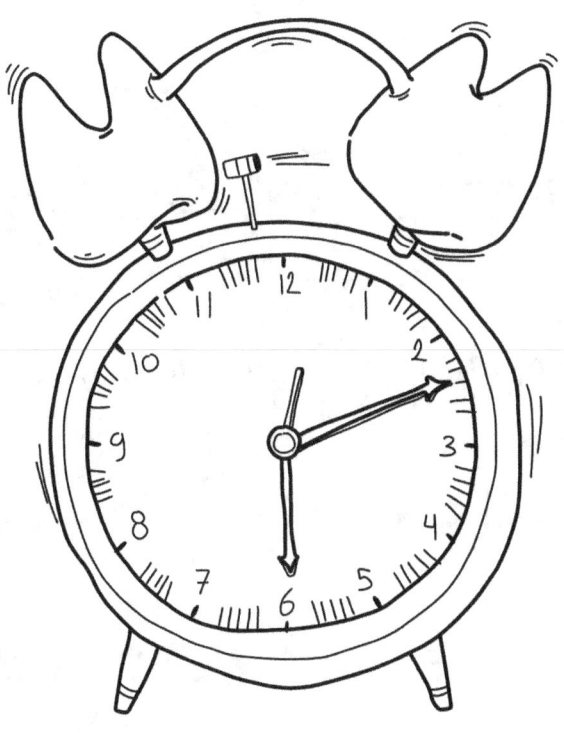

DID YOU HEAR ABOUT THE MAGIC TRACTOR?

FIRST OF ALL IT WENT DOWN THE ROAD, AND THEN SUDDENLY IT TURNED INTO A FIELD.

WHAT DO YOU CALL SOMEONE DRESSED UP AS SPAGHETTI?

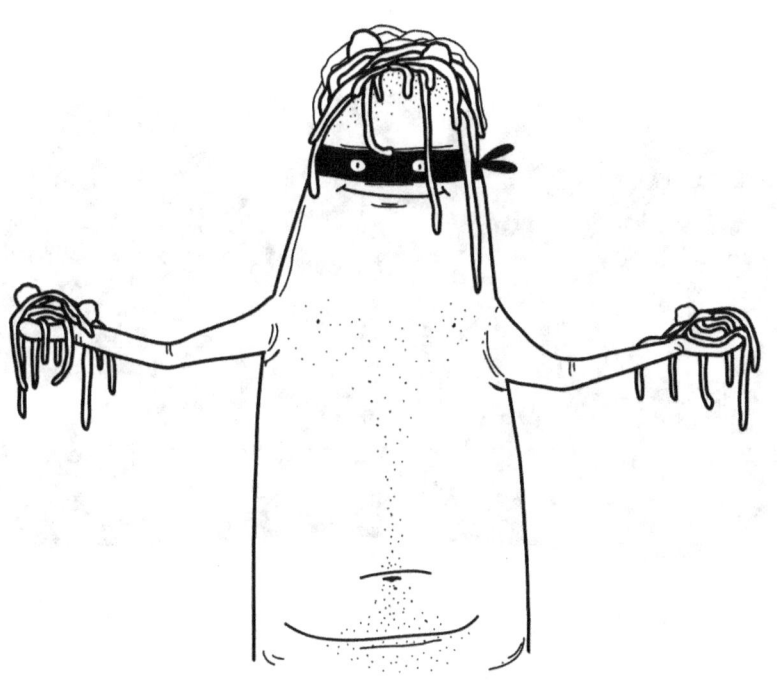

AN IMPASTA.

WHY DOES THE WORD "DARK" END WITH A k?

BECAUSE YOU CAN'T C IN THE DARK.

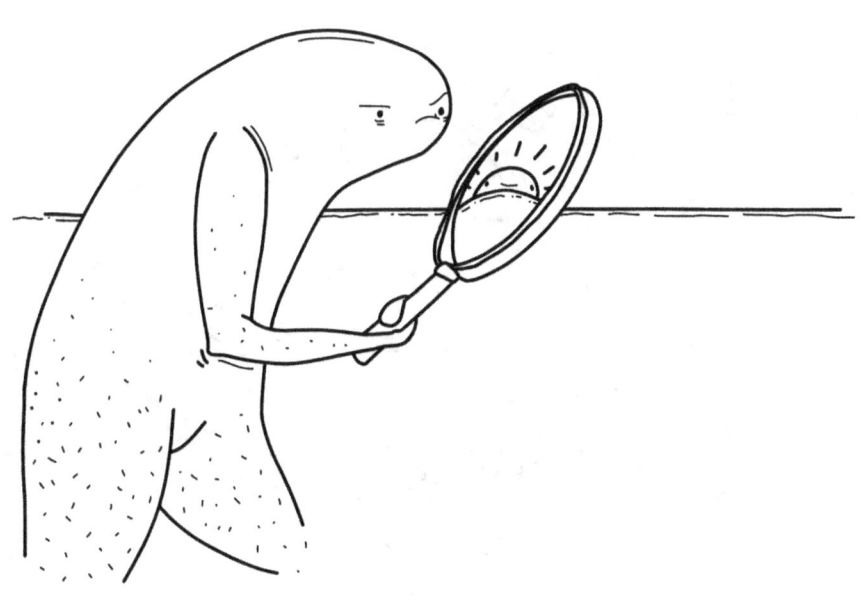

I FINALLY READ A BOOK ABOUT clocks.

It's about time.

WHY WAS THE INVENTION OF THE SPADE BIG NEWS?

BECAUSE IT WAS GROUNDBREAKING!

WHY SHOULDN'T YOU BUY VELCRO?

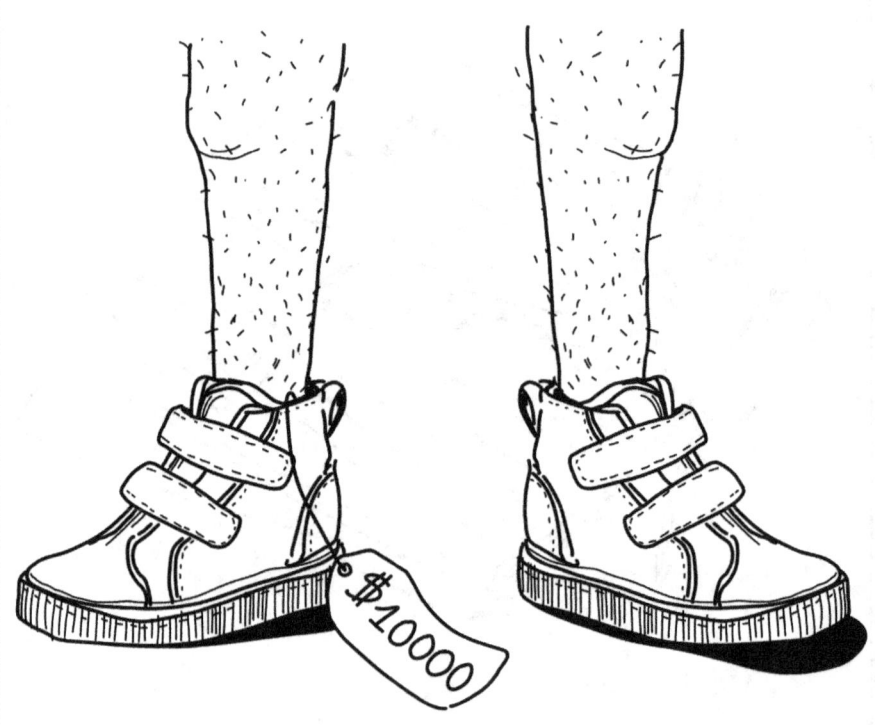

IT'S A RIP-OFF.

WHAT CLOTHES DOES A HOUSE WEAR?

ADDRESS.

WHY DON'T ANTS GET SICK?

BECAUSE THEY HAVE STRONG ANTY BODIES.

THERE WAS A FIRE AT THE CIRCUS.

it was in tents.

I TRIED TO MAKE A JOKE ABOUT MY JOB.

BUT I COULDN'T MAKE IT WORK.

WHAT DO YOU CALL TWO HORSES NEXT TO EACH OTHER?

NEIGH-BOURS.

WHY DID THE POLICE INTERVIEW THE SUSPECT IN AN OVEN?

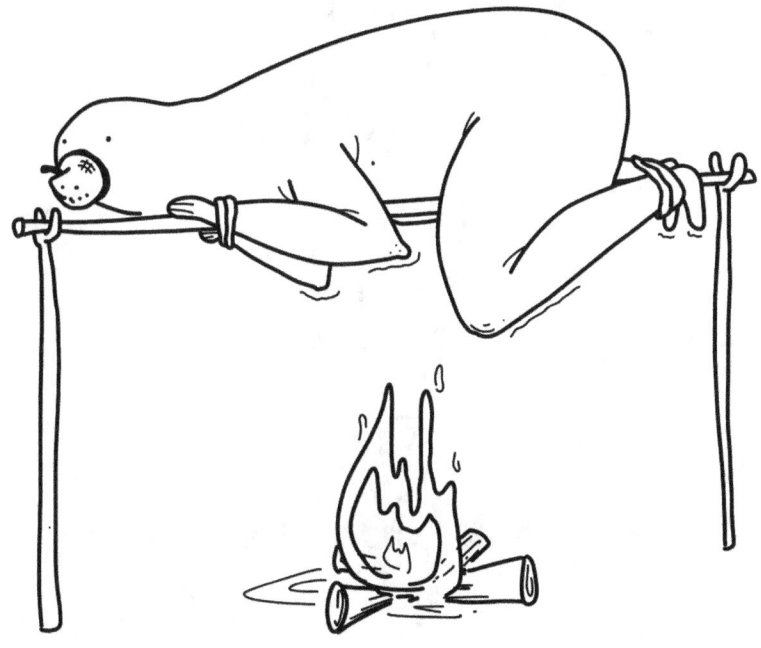

SO THEY COULD GRILL HIM.

A SCARECROW WON A NOBEL PRIZE.

It WAS BECAUSE HE WAS OUTSTANDING IN HIS FIELD.

I COULD tell you A joke ABOUT CHEDDAR.

BUT it's just too CHEESY!

IF I WAS GOING TO BE FRANK,

I'D HAVE TO CHANGE MY NAME

IF THE DEVIL WORE A WIG,

THERE'D BE HELL TOUPEE.

I ONLY UNDERSTAND 25 LETTERS
OF THE ALPHABET.

I CAN'T UNDERSTAND WHY.

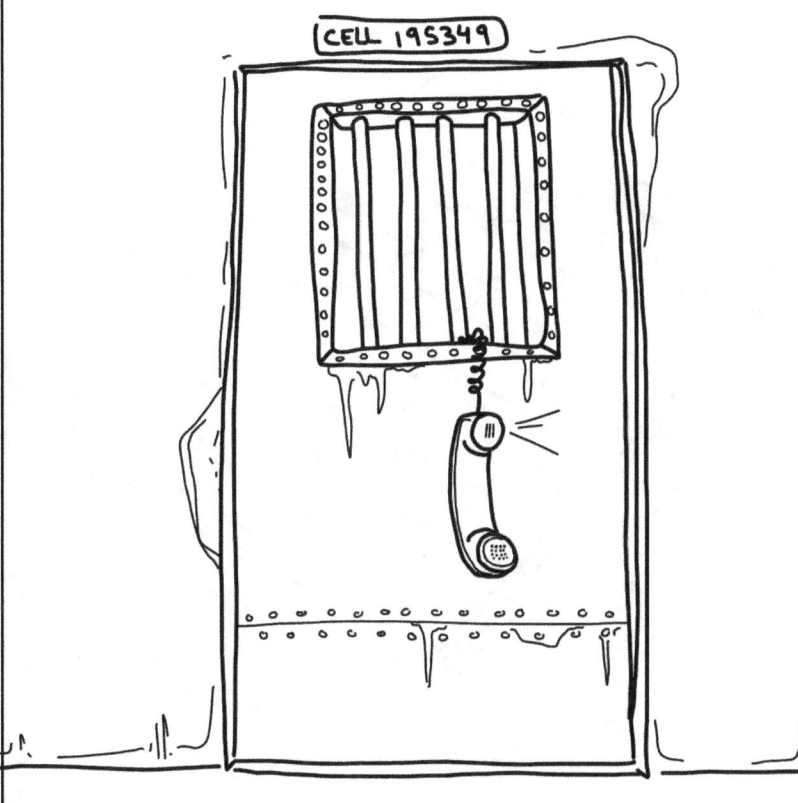

I BOUGHT A PEN THAT CAN WRITE UNDERWATER.

It CAN WRITE OTHER WORDS too.

WHY DID THE PONY DRINK WATER?

IT WAS A little HOARSE.

WHY ARE ROCK STARS COOL?

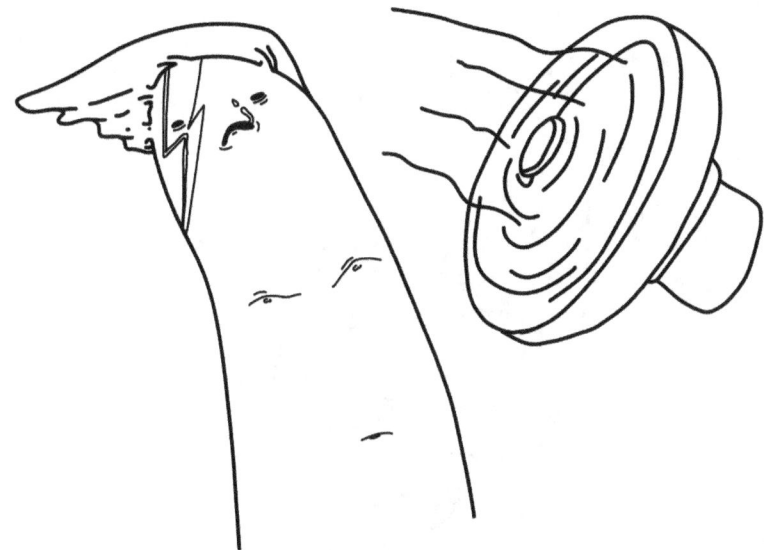

BECAUSE OF THEIR FANS.

WHAT IS THE BEST WAY TO MAKE A FARM GIRL LIKE YOU?

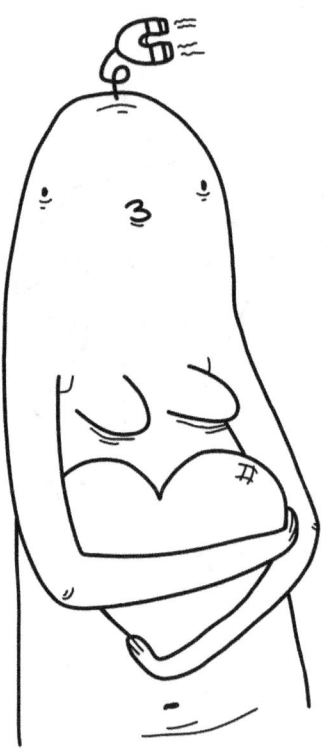

A TRACTOR.

WHAT IS THE POLITEST SEA IN FRANCE?

THE MERCI.

I HAD AN IDEA TO MAKE MY SNAIL FASTER BY TAKING HIS SHELL OFF.

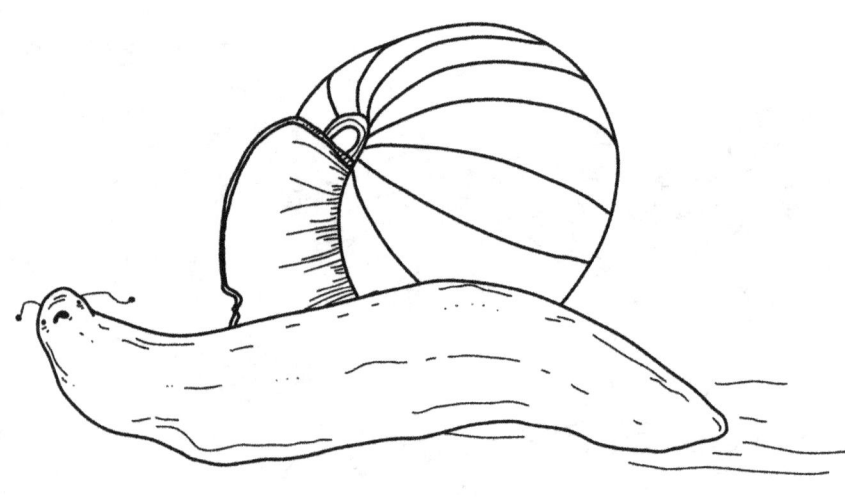

BUT IT JUST MADE HIM MORE SLUGGISH.

WHY DON'T COMMUNISTS USE TEA LEAVES?

BECAUSE PROPER TEA IS THEFT.

WHY WAS THE MAN WHO GREW HERBS BORED?

HE HAD too MUCH THYME ON HIS HANDS.

I WAS WATCHING A BASEBALL GAME THE OTHER DAY, AND I THOUGHT THE BALL WAS GETTING BIGGER.

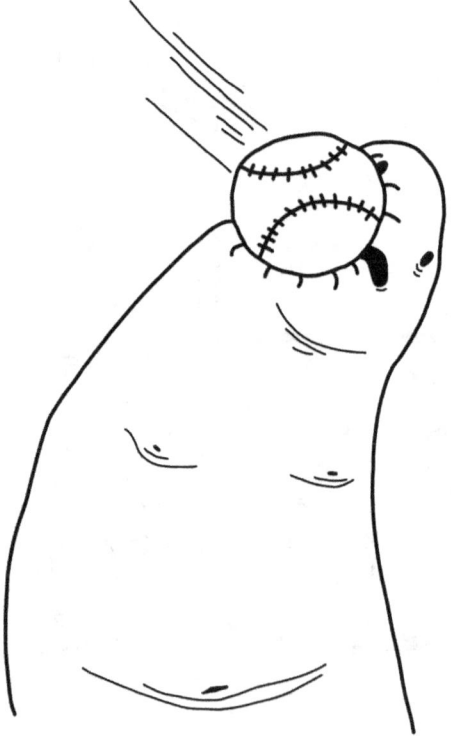

THEN IT HIT ME!

WHEN YOU ARE PLAYING CHESS, DON'T MOVE YOUR CASTLE TOO SOON.

THAT'S A ROOKIE MOVE.

I PAID $20 to GO AND SEE PRINCE.

BUT I PARTIED like it WAS $19.99

THE DOCTOR WANTED TO TAKE MY TEMPERATURE WITH A RECTAL THERMOMETER.

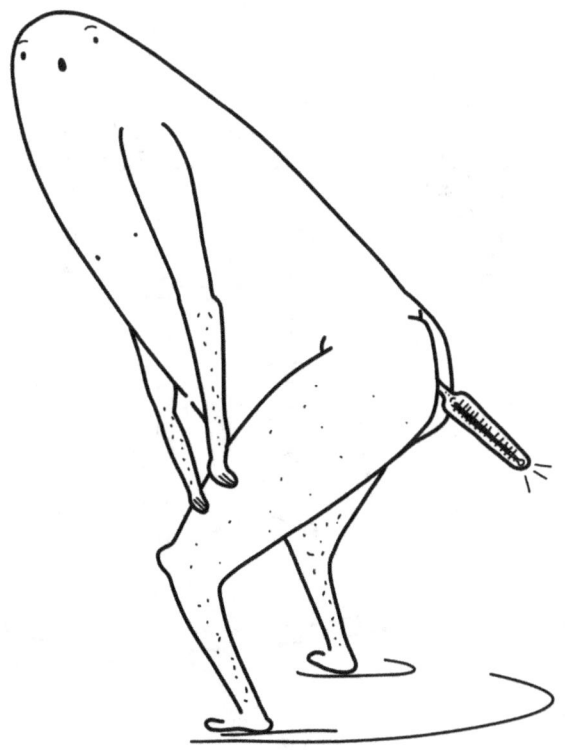

IT WAS A REAL PAIN IN THE ASS.

WHAT DO YOU SAY TO A SLEEPY CHILD WHO WON'T HAVE A NAP?

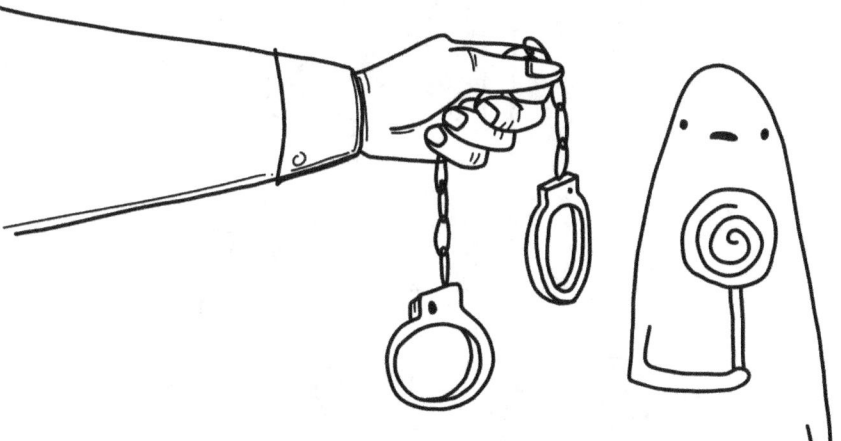

STOP RESISTING A REST!

I'M GOING TO THROW AWAY MY CALENDAR.

ITS DAYS ARE NUMBERED.

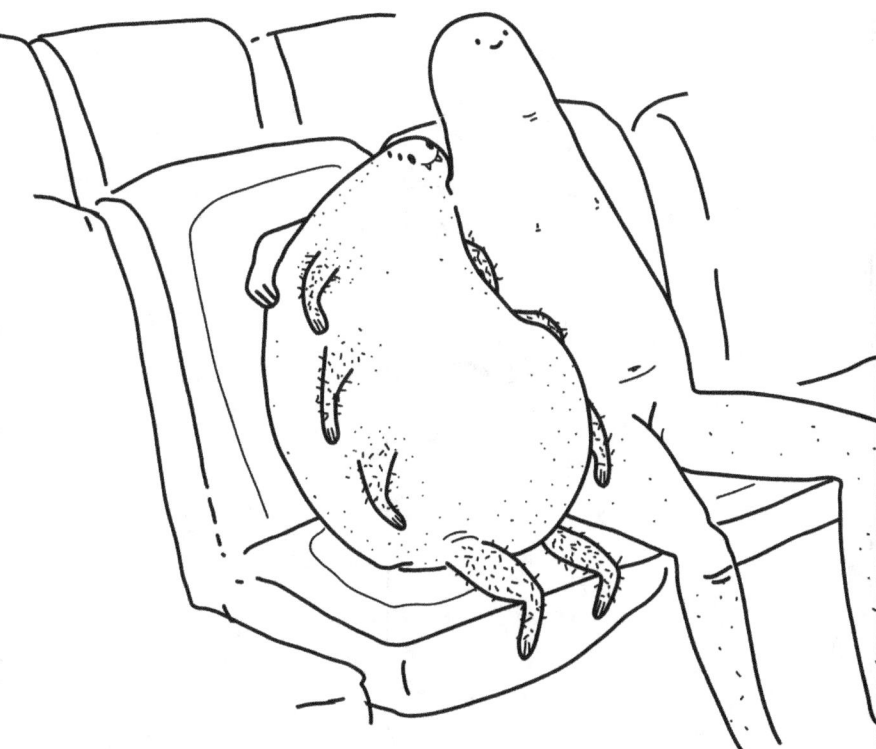

WHAT IS HEAVIER, A GALLON OF WATER OR A GALLON OF BUTANE?

BUTANE, it's lighter fluid.

I'M LEARNING HOW TO BUILD A STAIRCASE.

IT'S A STEP BY STEP PROCESS.

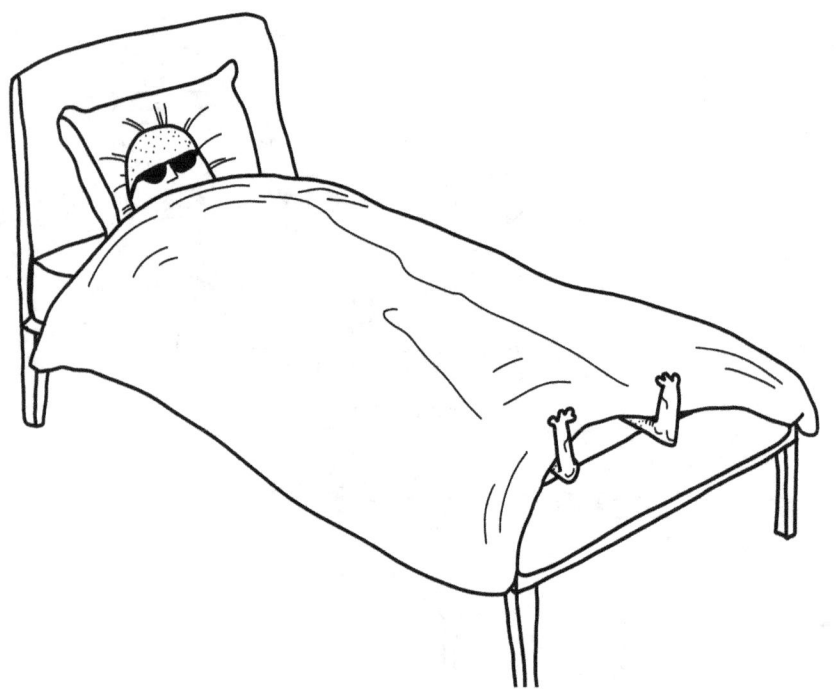

WHAT DO YOU CALL A MAGICIAN WHO GAVE UP MAGIC?

IAN.

WHY CAN'T YOU TRUST ATOMS?

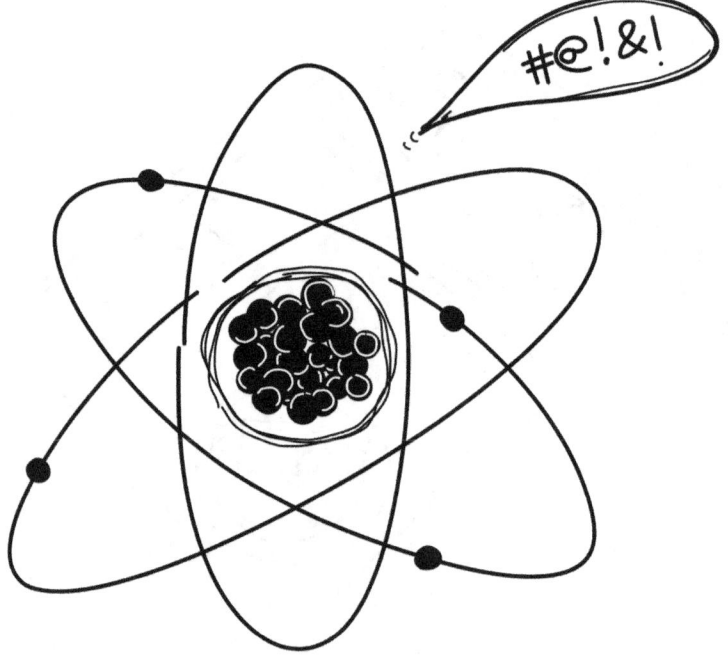

THEY MAKE UP EVERYTHING.

HOW DO YOU KNOW IF A CAKE IS SAD?

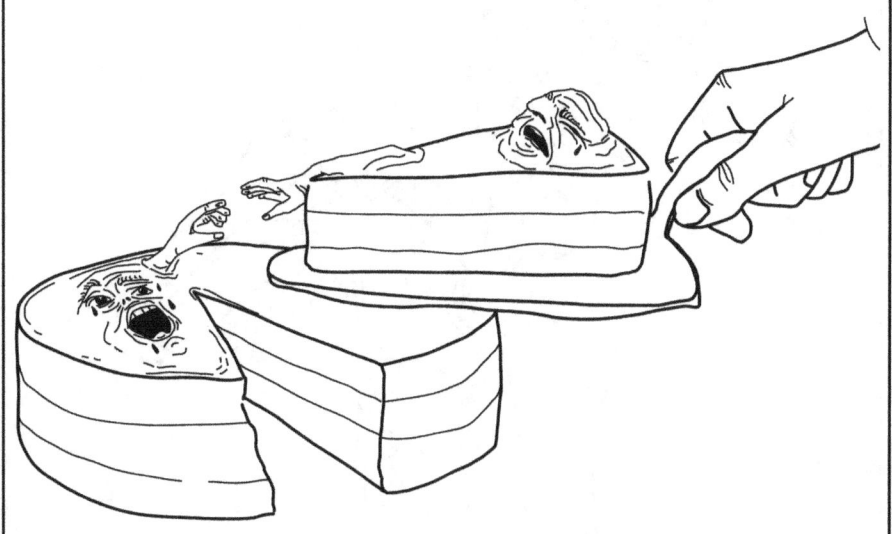

WHEN it's iN tiers.

WHY ARE MUSHROOMS ENTERTAINING?

BECAUSE THEY ARE FUN GUYS.

I GOT IN TROUBLE FOR HAVING AN INSTAGRAM MODEL ON TOP OF MY CAR.

THE POLICE SAID I WAS DRIVING UNDER THE INFLUENCER.

HOW DO YOU FEEl?

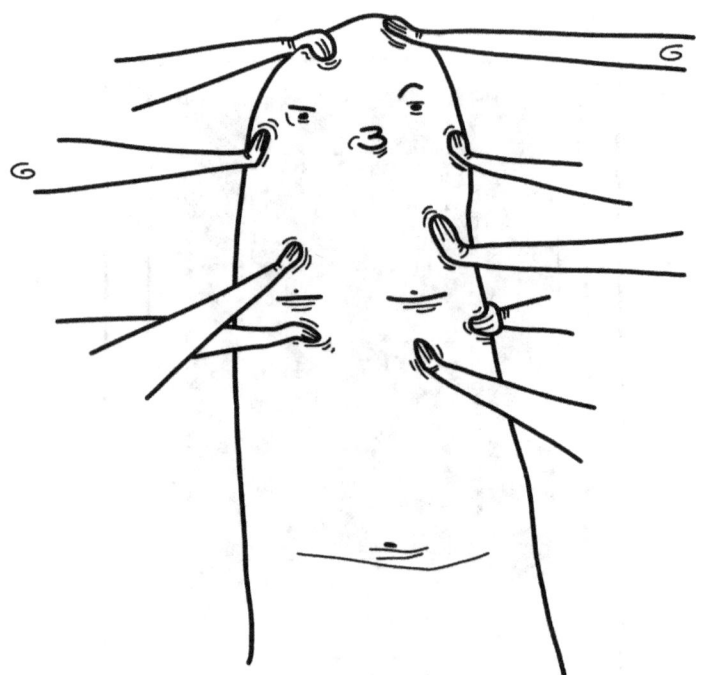

With your hands.

I MADE A BELT OUT OF HUNDRED DOLLAR BILLS.

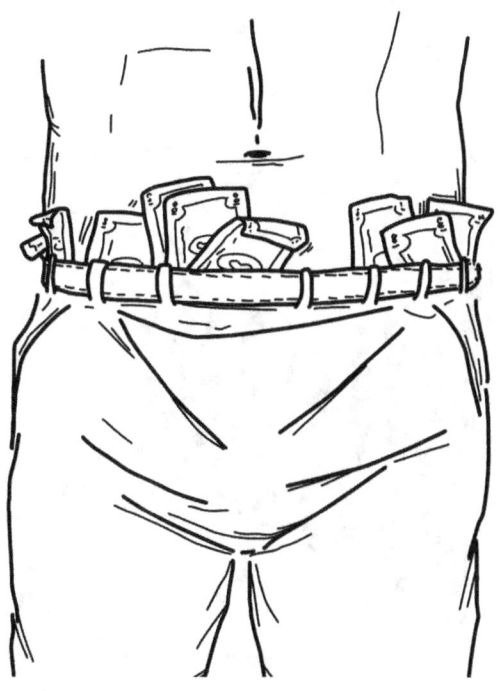

IT WAS A WAIST OF MONEY.

my wife told me to stop using my whistle inside.

but i blew it.

16 IS THE GREEDIEST NUMBER.

it's 8 AND 8.

I KNOW A JOKE ABOUT PAPER.

BUT IT'S TEARABLE.

I know a yacht builder who worked from home.

His sails went through the roof.

I TRIED TO MEMORIZE FIVE PAGES OF THE DICTIONARY.

I LEARNED NEXT TO NOTHING.

HOW DO YOU MAKE SEVEN EVEN?

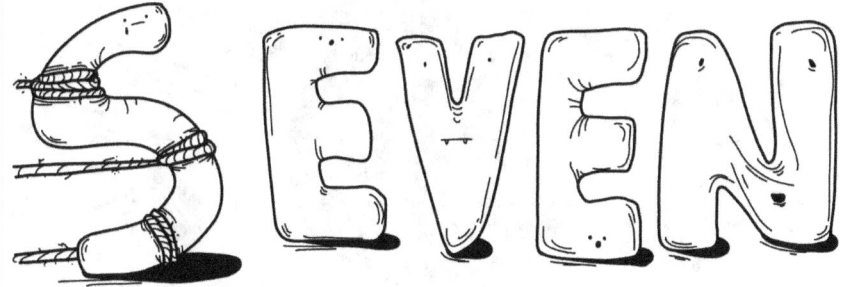

BY TAKING AWAY THE S.

He best jokes are about eyes.

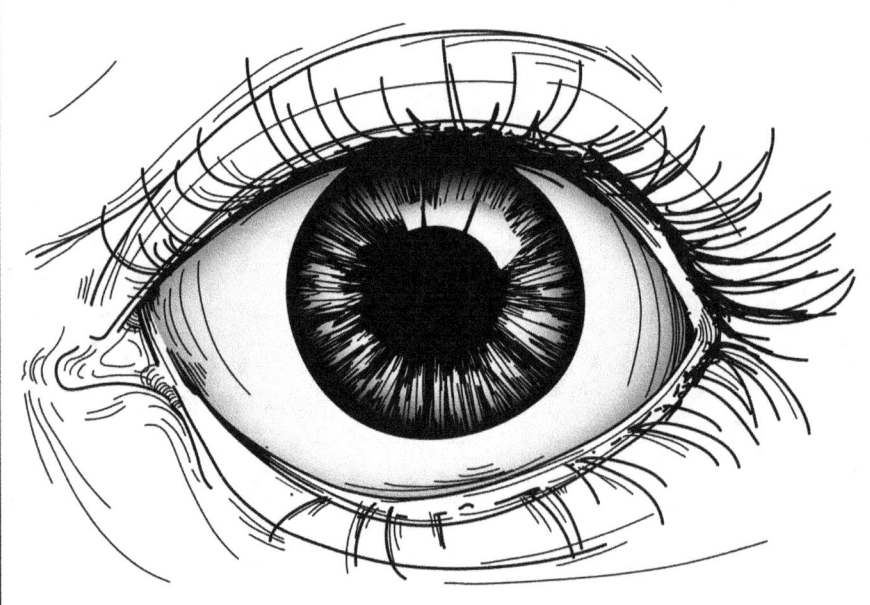

THE CORNEA, THE BETTER!

DID YOU HEAR ABOUT THE NIGHT CLUB ON THE MOON?

IT HAD NO ATMOSPHERE.

A BEAR WALKS INTO A BAR AND SAYS, "ONE BEER AND............ONE VODKA." THE BARMAN SAYS, "WHY THE BIG PAUSE?"

THE BEAR REPLIES, "I DON'T KNOW. I WAS BORN WITH THEM LIKE THAT."

WHAT'S THE LEAST SPOKEN LANGUAGE IN THE WORLD?

SIGN LANGUAGE.

WHY DO BEES HUM?

BECAUSE THEY DON'T KNOW THE WORDS.

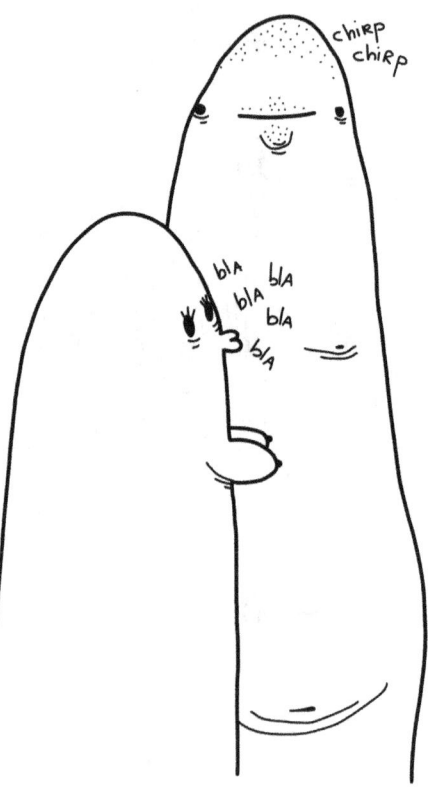

Why shouldn't you eat too much tropical fruit?

Because it can make a mango crazy.

WHAt HAPPENED to tHE iNVENtOR OF tHE "knock-knock" jokE?

HE WON A NO BEll PRIZE.

Icy is the easiest word to spell.

Looking at it, I see why.

I SAW GLORIA GAYNOR'S GHOST LAST NIGHT.

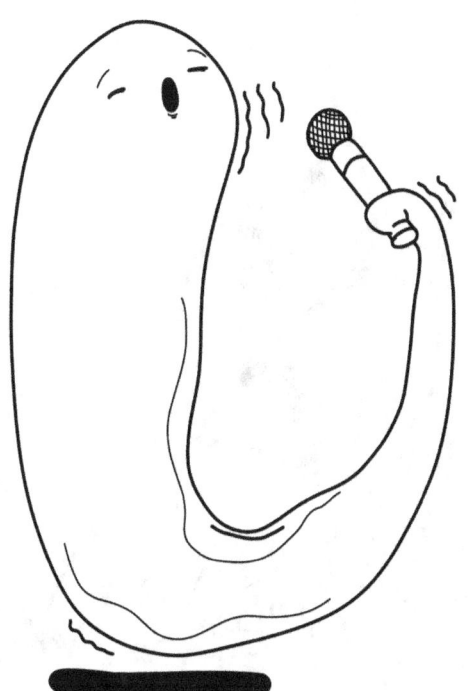

FIRST I WAS AFRAID, I WAS PETRIFIED.

WHY CAN'T VIKINGS WRITE?

WHENEVER THEY TRY, THEY RUNE IT.

DO YOU KNOW WHAT A STARVING HIPPO IN BUDAPEST IS CALLED?

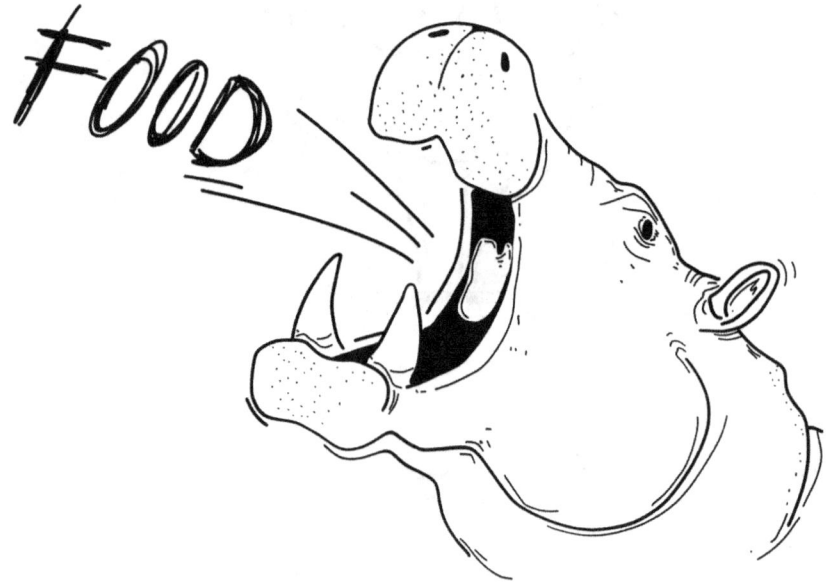

A HUNGARY, HUNGRY HIPPO.

What do you call it when a kitchen utensil farts?

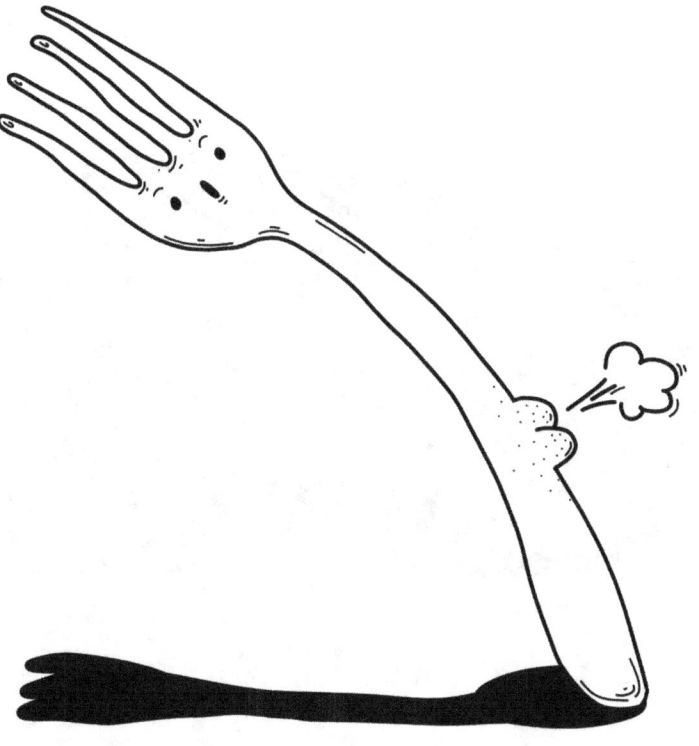

Spatulence.

WHAT WORKS BETTER WHEN it's tired?

A CAR.

WHY ARE THERE ONLY THREE LEGS ON MILKING STOOLS?

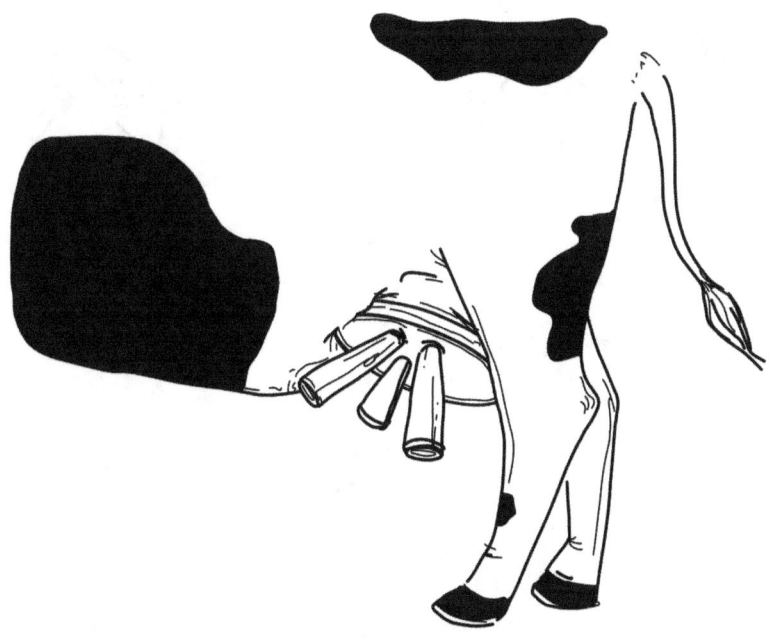

BECAUSE THE COW HAS THE UDDER.

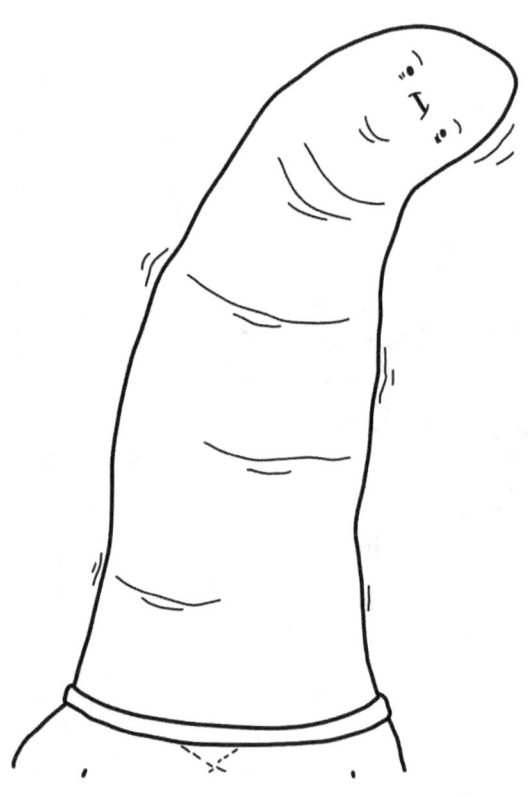

HOW DO GHOSTS GET DRUNK?

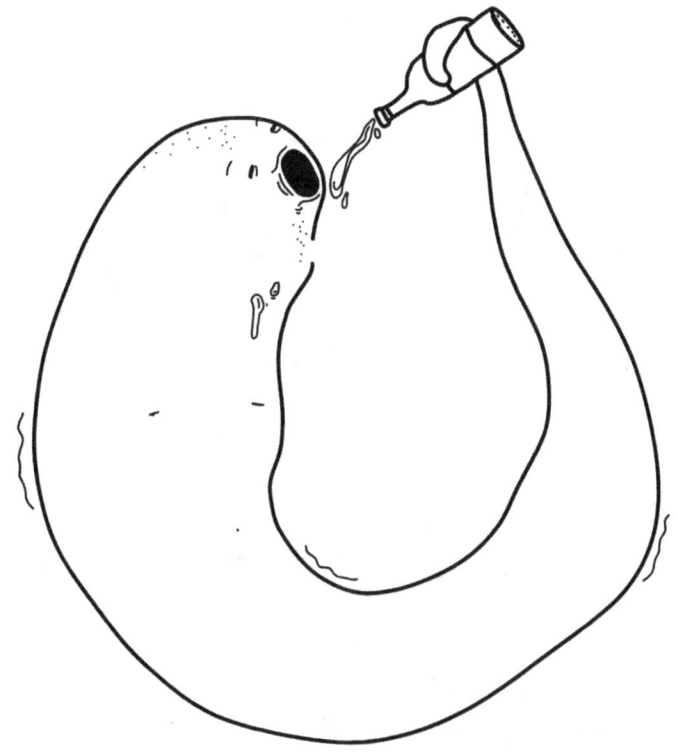

BOOZE.

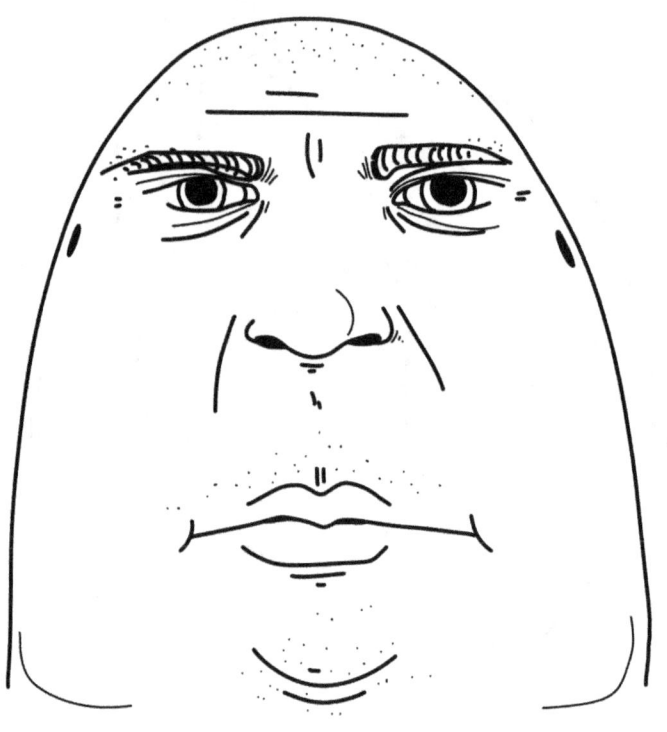

DID YOU HEAR ABOUT THE INAPPROPRIATE GAMES CONSOLE?

IT SAID THINGS IT DIDN'T NINTENDO.

I WANTED TO GIVE ARCHERY A SHOT.

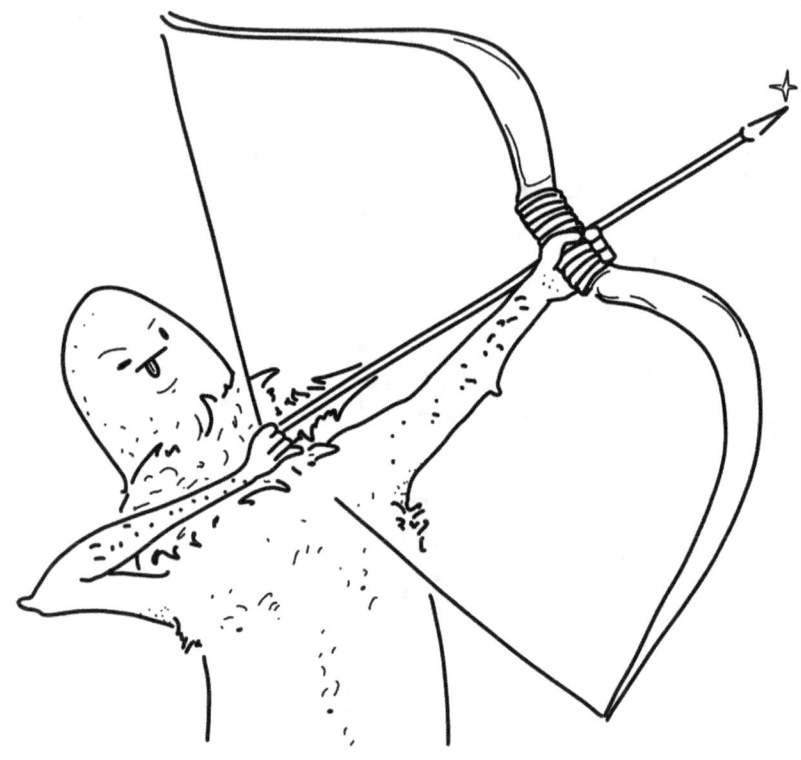

BUT THERE ARE A LOT OF DRAWBACKS.

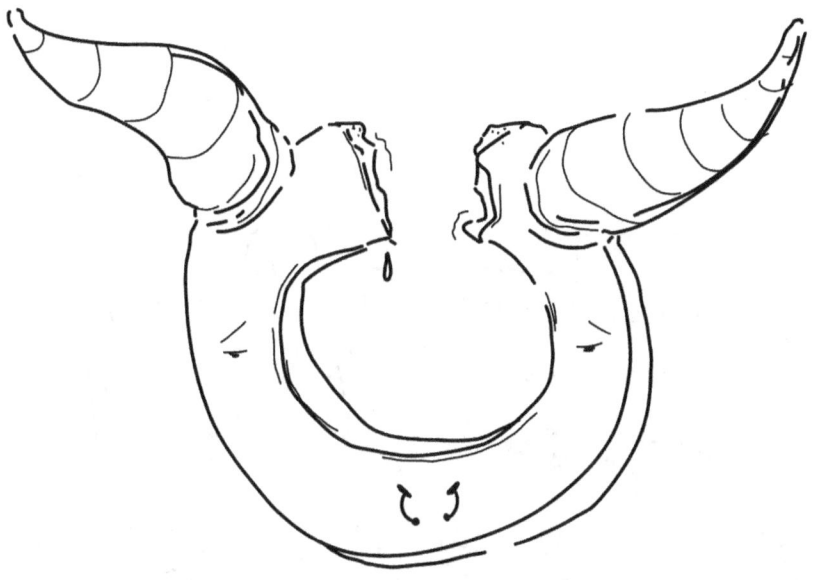

what's the best tea for a model?

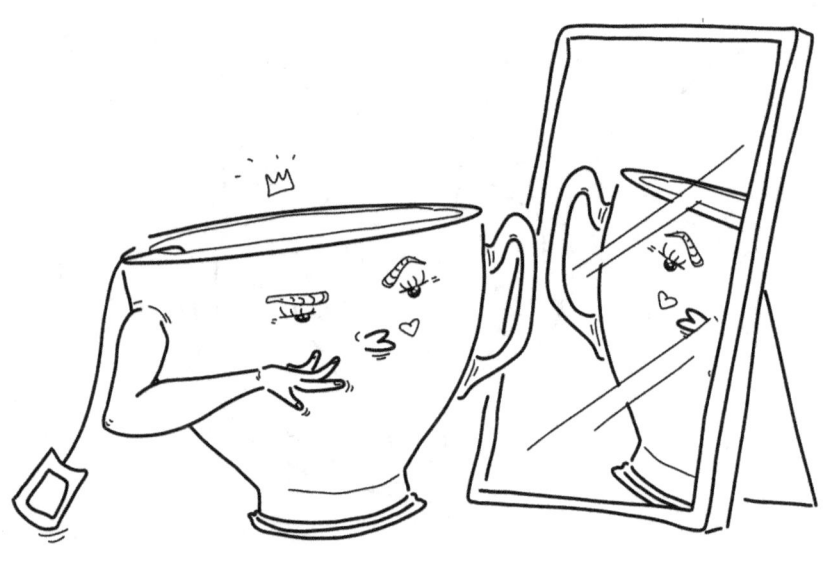

vanity.

it took me a while to learn subtraction.

BUT I LEARNED THAT LESSEN.

www.ingramcontent.com/pod-product-compliance
Lightning Source LLC
Chambersburg PA
CBHW071407080526
44587CB00017B/3203